MW00724103

Babies are born with hearts of gold

pictures and verse
by

Sandra Magsamen

gift

stewart tabori & chang

Babies come to earth filled with gifts uniquely their own.

These cherished
pieces of heaven
are the purest
form of love
that is known.

With tiny little hands they touch our hearts forever...

their cheerful little smiles are sweet and their laughter delights with pleasure.

Each little
miracle
with an
angel's
face . . .

gives us renewed belief in the potential and grace of the human race.

Shower them
with hugs
and kisses
and listen to
them well...

You will be astonished by the stories they will tell.

Tell them
they are
special, perfect
in wonderful
ways.

Laugh and
play in the
sun's bright
rays...

watch as they explore and discover their individual ways.

Sing the songs of childhood — "Ring Around the "Rosie" and sleepy lullabies . . .

rock them in your arms as they drift into their dreams and close their little eyes.

Be honored
you're a parent
chosen to
guide this soul
along the way.

above all
tell them
that you
love them each
and every day.

Pictures and verse by Sandra Magsamen
© 2000 Hanny Girl Productions, Inc.
Exclusive licensing agent Momentum Partners, Inc., NY, NY

Published in 2000 by
Stewart, Tabori & Chang
A division of U.S. Media Holdings, Inc.
115 West 18th Street
New York, NY 10011

Distributed in Canada by
General Publishing Company Ltd.
30 Lesmill Road
Don Mills, Ontario, Canada M3B 2T6

ISBN: 1-58479-004-0

Printed in Hong Kong

10 9 8 7 6 5 4 3 2 1